Autumn Days

Autumn poems for children

Hadley James

Autumn Days

Hadley James

Contents

Seasons

Spring, summer, autumn, winter,
Winter, autumn, summer, spring,
Each season has a character,
And magic that they bring.

Spring means new beginnings,
Everything begins to grow,
The earth wakes from its slumber,
Snowdrops start to show.

The days start getting lighter,
The sun returns and then,
The daffodils spread sunshine,
The plants wake up again.

Summer is the time for fun,
The days are long and bright,
Time for picnics and ice creams,
The evenings are so light.

It's time for endless holidays,
For visits to the beach,
Days filled with possibilities,
From Summer's endless reach.

Autumn is time to reflect,
To let go and renew,
The school year is beginning,
The harvest is reaped too.

The trees are shedding all their leaves,
It's time for Halloween,
There are bonfires and fireworks,
Making up an autumn dream.

Winter is time to hibernate,
To be indoors and warm,
We celebrate the season,
And watch for a snowstorm.

It's time to get together,
For parties, fun and laughter,
To look forward to the new year,
And our Happy Ever After.

Autumn Questions

How do you know it is autumn?
What does it mean to you?
When it gets to autumn?
What do you like to do?

Do you like the falling leaves?
Do you like to collect conkers?
Do you like it when it's cold?
Or does it drive you bonkers?

Do you like the Harvest Festival?
A chance to give our thanks.
Do you like to walk through autumn woods?
Or along the river banks?

Do you like the smell of bonfire smoke
Drifting in the air?
Do you dress up for Halloween?
With cobwebs in your hair?

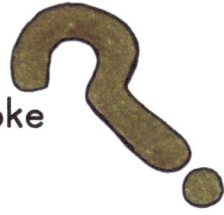

Do you like to snuggle up
All safe and warm and cosy?
Do you like to drink hot chocolate?
Until you're tired and dozy?

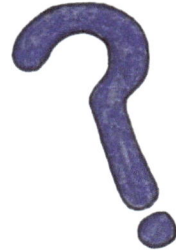

What do you like about autumn?
What does it mean to you?
Is it your favourite season?
What do you like to do?

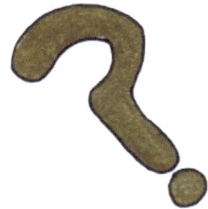

Autumn Begins

The farmer gathers the harvest,
Squirrels collect acorns and nuts,
Hedgehogs get ready to have a long sleep,
The hay in the field is cut.

The days are getting shorter,
A nip of cold in the air,
Mornings and evenings are darker,
Bonfire smoke floats everywhere.

We collect the shiny smooth conkers,
We kick through the leaves on the floor,
The trees are looking bare,
Hats and scarves come out once more.

The clocks fall back to save the day,
We carve out pumpkin lights,
Bonfires and fireworks light up the sky,
Brightening the autumn night.

September Start

September is here,
My pencil case is new,
The school year begins,
A fresh start for me and you.

My shoes are shiny,
My uniform is pressed,
It feels so grown up,
When I am dressed.

A different teacher,
A brand new class,
New things to learn,
And tests to pass.

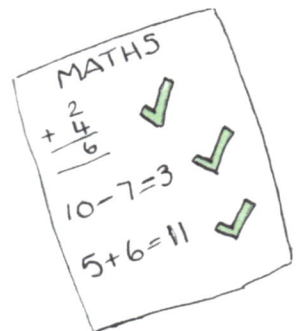

We know the routine by the end of the week,
We're happy the weekend is here,
We worked really hard, now it's time for fun,
We all give a great big cheer.

Questions Before School

What time do we have to get there?
Which one is my door?
Will my teacher like me?
Do I have to sit on the floor?

Will we do painting?
Will we read books?
Can I play outside?
Will we play with cars and trucks?

When will we have lunch?
Will there be good things to eat?
Will I make lots of friends?
Will I like the people I meet?

Will we have a story?
Will there be a bell that rings?
Will there be computers?
Will I have to sing?

When will it be home time?
Is it in the afternoon?
Can I go again tomorrow?
I want to go back soon!

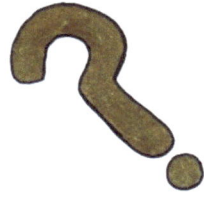

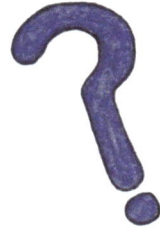

Amazing Autumn

There is something about Autumn,
That I really do adore,
When the leaves jump dancing from the trees,
And the cold knocks on the door.

The nights are getting darker,
The mornings crisp and bright,
When fireworks light the sky,
It fills me with delight.

Autumn Leaves

Red, orange, yellow, brown,
The Autumn leaves come tumbling down,
You can see them all around,
They crunch and scrunch on the ground.

Magenta, green, purple, gold,
The air is crisp and getting cold,
The wind blows until the trees are bare,
Autumn leaves are everywhere.

Harvest

H is for the hay all yellow, cut and bound.

A is for the apples that are falling to the ground.

R is for the rows of crops to gather and collect.

V is for the vegetables the farmers all inspect.

E is for excitement for a delicious feast.

S is for smiling as the harvest has increased.

T is for thankful for farmers and all they do.

Let's celebrate the harvest and the food for me and you.

Autumn Art

All around leaves swirl and dance,

Under feet they sometimes prance,

Twirling gently on the breeze,

Untamed they leap away from trees,

Majestically they ride the air,

Nature's art for us to share.

Harvest Festival

I've packed my basket,
It's arranged with care,
I'm excited for the festival,
I hope Mum will be there.

We all go in the hall,
Put our baskets down,
Vegetables and fruits,
The best display in town.

We sit in our lines,
Then we wait our turn,
Listen to the songs and poems,
My stomach starts to churn.

Then it's my class,
I say my lines loud,
Mum gives me a wave,
I can see she is proud.

We sing all the songs,
Our voices sound so sweet,
The Mums, Dads and Grannies,
Say it's a lovely treat.

Then we give our thanks,
For the harvest and the food,
Our Headteacher is smiling,
She's in a good mood.

Everyone claps,
We all take a bow,
The food will be donated,
To the foodbank now.

Remember to give thanks,
When you're having a rest,
To have so much food,
We really are blessed.

Conkers

Shiny jewels fall to the ground,
Hiding, waiting to be found,
Hunting for this Autumn treasure,
Really is the greatest pleasure.

Find them, admire them, then take them home,
Special delights that are yours alone,
Count them, display them or use them to play,
Or plant them so they'll be a tree some day.

Autumn Colours

Brown shiny conkers fall to the ground,
Yellow is the scarecrow who guards all around,
Red bonfire flames light up the night,
Orange leaves are a beautiful sight,
Golden corn is being cut,
Green crunchy leaves are underfoot,
Beige is the wheat that has grown just right,
Silver webs sparkle on a frosty night,
All these colours and so many more,
Tell us that autumn knocks on the door.

Scarecrow

I stand all alone in the field,
Wearing my hat with pride,
I waggle my arms when the wind blows,
It makes birds fly and hide.

The smile is fixed upon my face,
I wish that I could dance,
I can only move when the wind blows,
It is my only chance.

I'm wearing a blue jacket,
My hands are made of straw,
The gardeners all adore me,
The plants are safe once more!

Pumpkin Carving

We go and choose them carefully,
To find the perfect one,
Not too big and not too small,
For pumpkin carving fun.

We cut a hole in the top,
And scoop out all the pulp,
We save the seeds to plant them,
Then get our tools to sculpt.

We carve a zigzag mouth,
A triangle for the nose,
Stars for two pumpkin eyes,
This is the way we chose.

Pumpkin carving is an art,
To brighten up the night,
Create your funny face,
Then fill it with magical light.

Halloween Party

The witches and ghosties and goblins
come out,
It's dark and they all want to play,
The cobwebs are coating the houses,
Because it's Halloween today.

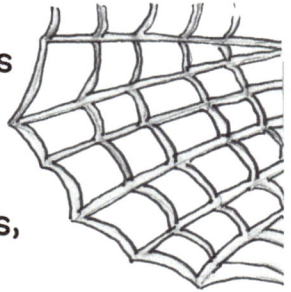

It's time to dress up and celebrate,
To apple bob and have fun,
People have fancy dress parties,
Trick or treating has begun.

We tell ghost and spooky stories,
We drink potions and witches' brew,
To celebrate the season,
Wearing costumes that are new.

Halloween is a spooky day,
To give our friends a fright,
A time to get together,
When it's dark at night.

Diwali

A long time ago, Prince Rama lived,
With Sita his beautiful wife,
The people all adored them,
They lived a happy life.

That is until disaster struck,
The King sent them away,
They went to live in a forest,
And Rama's brother came to stay.

Living nearby was a demon king,
Ravana was his name,
He had ten heads and twenty arms,
Everyone feared his games.

Ravana kidnapped Sita,
Taking her away,
She left a trail of jewels,
So Rama would know the way.

Rama and his brother,
Followed Sita's trail,
When they met the Monkey King,
They knew they could not fail.

Hanuman the monkey king,
Sent messages far and wide,
The monkeys went to find Sita,
Ravana could not hide!

Hanuman found Sita,
On an island hard to reach,
They began to build a bridge,
To take them to the beach.

When the bridge was built,
They rushed without a thought,
They reached Ravana's kingdom,
And a huge battle was fought.

Rama killed Ravana,
With his bow and magic arrow,
The whole world rejoiced,
It bought an end to all their sorrow.

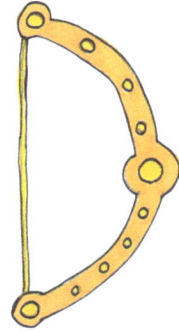

Rama and Sita were reunited,
They began their journey home,
People lit lamps to guide the way,
To show they weren't alone.

Every year at Diwali,
The lamps are lit once more,
To show that light beats darkness,
For now and evermore.

Let's Celebrate Diwali!

Hooray, hooray Diwali is here,
Time to celebrate,
We all have lots of things to do,
It's going to be great!

First, we clean our home,
And buy new clothes to wear,
We get lots of clay diyas,
To have light everywhere.

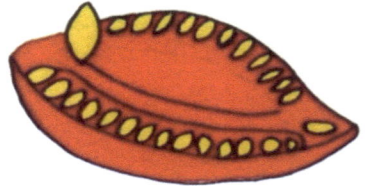

We make rangoli patterns,
They are colourful and bright,
They decorate the entrance,
To welcome the goddess of light.

We prepare food and sweets,
The house is decorated too,
Then we visit the Temple together,
It's fun for me and you.

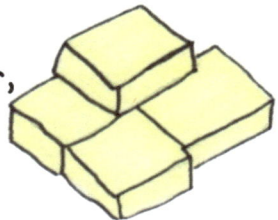

We offer sweets to goddess Lakshmi,
Decorate the temple all around,
We put diyas by the windows,
So the light helps us be found.

Now it's time for home,
We tell stories and we feast,
We think about Rama and Sita,
And Ravana the ten headed beast.

We enjoy the yummy food,
Pakoras, samosas and sweets,
Then it is time for fireworks,
So many party treats!

Bonfire

The smoke swirls upwards through the air,
It dances on my clothes and hair,
The fire burns bright, flames of orange and red,
Warm my hands and body and head.

We have baked potatoes and hot dogs to eat,
Then toffee apples and parkin for a treat,
The night is dark, there's a chill in the air,
 The fire keeps us warm so we don't care!

Fireworks Display

A thousand stars light up the sky,
The rockets zoom and whoosh and fly,

A rainbow of colour lights up the night,
A wonderful, truly amazing sight.

A happy crowd says "Ooh" and "Ahh,"
This is the best display by far.

Everyone is wrapped up tight,
Cosy in the Autumn night,

The fireworks crash and whizz and bang,
"What a show!" The crowd all sang.

Thanksgiving

It's time to give thanks and remember,
Time to gather the family round,
To think of all our blessings,
And give thanks for them out loud.

The table is laid, the feast is set,
Roast turkey and cornbread,
Candied yams and pumpkin pie,
It's such an amazing spread.

It's time to remember the Fathers,
Adventurers exploring the new,
Looking for places to start new lives,
And making their dreams come true.

So we say thank you for the harvest,
Thanks for family and for friends,
We count our blessings one by one,
And hope they never end.

Autumn Days

A ll around the leaves fall down,

U nder bushes, feet and trees,

T hey tumble and twirl in the wind,

U niquely dancing with the breeze.

M ornings are getting darker,

N ights are drawing in,

D ays feel so much shorter,

A nd the cold tickles our skin,

Y ellow corn is harvested, it's time to celebrate,

S o enjoy the days of Autumn, they really are so great!

Sleep Tight

An Autumn chill bites the air,
The squirrel collects his nuts with care,
He gathers twigs and leaves and food,
To keep him warm and feed his brood.

The hedgehog prepares and starts to get cosy,
The Autumn weather makes her feel dozy,
She snuggles down getting ready to sleep,
And wakes when spring bulbs begin to peep.

Lantern Parade

A thousand lights dance in the night,
A sea of faces and sheer delight.

I can't wait to see the different styles,
Created with love and bringing smiles.

The lights dance as we walk around,
The crowd gasps and makes a clapping sound.

We parade in the winter night,
The twinkling lights a wondrous sight.

Carols are sung, a joyous sound,
Peace and love is all around.

Also by Hadley James:

Wonderful Me
Hadley James

Horrid Halloween
Hadley James

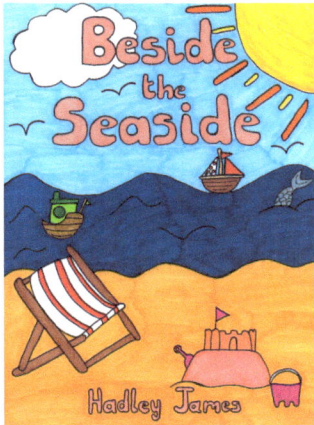
Beside the Seaside
Hadley James

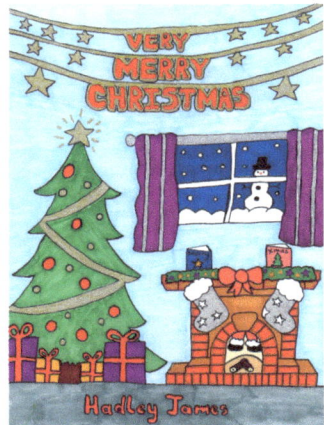
VERY MERRY CHRISTMAS
Hadley James

Wonderful Winter

Hadley James

Spectacular Spring

Hadley James

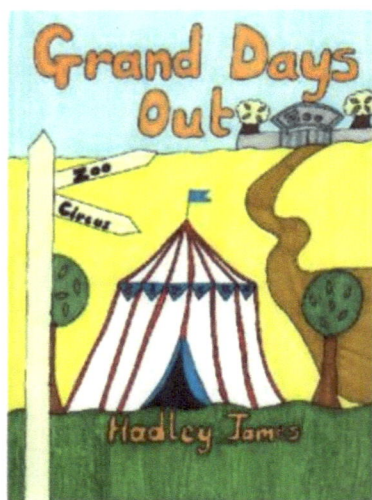

Grand Days Out

Zoo

Circus

Hadley James

Extreme Environments

Hadley James

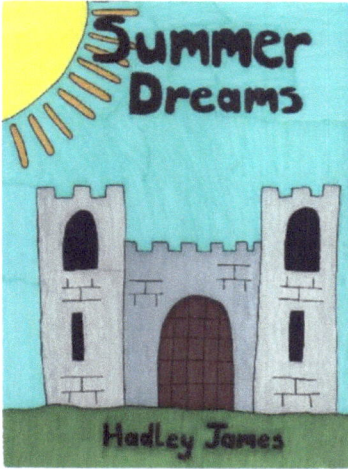

Summer
Dreams

Hadley James

Marvellous
Minibeasts

Hadley James

Fabulous
Farm

Hadley James

www.ingramcontent.com/pod-product-compliance
Lightning Source LLC
Chambersburg PA
CBHW040145070426
42448CB00032B/20